Blue Sparrow

Tweets on Writing, Reading, and Other Creative Nonsense

by Ksenia Anske @kseniaanske

© Copyright 2013 by Ksenia Anske
http://www.kseniaanske.com/

This work is made available under the terms of the
Creative Commons Attribution-NonCommercial-ShareAlike 3.0 license,
http://creativecommons.org/licenses/by-nc-sa/3.0/

ISBN: 978-0615823607

Tweet is a trademark of Twitter Inc. This book is not endorsed or sponsored by Twitter.

There are only three things I do.
I read. I write. And I fart glitter.

Run around. Jump. Scream your head off. Be as immature as you can. That's what life is about. And when you're done running, WRITE.

If while writing your novel you decide it's SHIT, don't quit, keep writing till you're done. All 1st drafts are shit by definition.

Letter by letter, word by word, sentence by sentence, page by page. It's that easy to write, and that hard.

Write anything and everything, because it's much better than writing nothing.

I'm weird. On the surface I look quiet and composed, but inside I have a hundred voices raging at full volume.

Write without holding back. Write as if you've grown wings and are flying for the first time. Write like living your last day. Write.

The most important part of writing may be the simple step of not rewriting everything you did the day before, but to keep moving forward.

Writing is an amazing thing.
Because paper doesn't tell you to
shut up, never ever EVER.

Everything has been said already.
But it hasn't been said the way
you'd say it. So go ahead. WRITE.

It's hard to walk when your legs are wobbly, but you learned. It's hard to write when your words are wobbly, but you'll learn.
KEEP AT IT.

Does world seem black and white to you? Read books. You will see color.

A poor attempt at writing is better than no attempt at all.

The only way to really learn how to write is by doing it.

Just forget the world and its naysayers. Close the door and write. Let them talk while you're building your future.

If there is a hole inside you, stuff it with books. They will stop the bleeding.

I live on the mountain of my madness, on the very top.

If books aren't magic, then I don't know what is.

If I didn't write, I'd explode in a brilliant shower of literacy sparkles and would be no more.

There are no rules to writing except one. KEEP WRITING.

A writer can't not write. If a writer can't write, a writer will bite.

Writing makes you happy, then keeps you happy, then immortalizes your happiness forever.

To write better dialogue, I turned into an eavesdropper.

The exhilaration from finishing your 1st book compares maybe only to being in love for the 1st time, your heart all aflutter and melting.

Above all, write. Your story will sell itself.

Writing is breathing life into forgotten memories.

A great book is the one you dive in and swim until there is no air left, but you keep swimming, forgetting air, breathing the story.

Writing is not about winning awards, writing is about winning hearts.

Who is happy sitting alone at home, reading a book, smiling like a lunatic? A WRITER.

A dead crow has pecked out all my thoughts and left my head an empty husk of nonsense.

Why is reading important?
Because it gives you a fresh
perspective on your own writing.

The only thing I'm sure about is this. I WANT TO KEEP WRITING.

There is no such thing as crazy writing. What's crazy is NOT to write.

Read, and you'll see a million skies.

Your worry days are over. You're a writer. Worry on paper.

I know it feels like it, but you're not alone in your pain. Shed it. Write a story. And we'll tell you that our pain is the same.

Writers are introverts that know how to talk.

I'm not spacing out, I'm writing in my head.

True horror is not in our stories, it's in our lives. Stories help us process it.

Reading is the best medicine,
writing is the best cure.

Everyone who tells you that you can't write, write them into a novel. I think it would make for a great cocktail of characters.

Every time I read the news, I know the only thing I can do is keep writing like crazy, to maybe change the world for the better.

Hey, you, aspiring writer, stop aspiring and start WRITING already!

Writers are those weird people that like to take off their skin in public.

Write. Once you start, you won't be able to stop. Trust me.

The only way to get better at writing is... *drumroll*
...TO KEEP WRITING!

Writing empties. Reading fills.

Writing nonsense frees me to write sense.

Stop dreaming about writing.
WRITE. Dreams will follow.

You have a story inside you.
LET. IT. OUT.

Writers are simply those people that learned to process their pain by writing.

I'm addicted to words, so I write.

Why do writers need to sleep? It's very inconvenient.

Books are merely translations of our emotions into words that allow us to connect on an almost blood transfusion level.

There are entire universes in your mind, if you only dare to look inside.

Reading gives me courage to keep writing.

Writers wear their hearts on the pages of their books.

Writers don't sleep. Writers keep writing in their heads while they're dreaming.

A good story is the one that makes you forget you're reading a story.

Never compromise. Write it as it is. Always.

Your curse is yourself. You're the biggest obstacle you will ever have to battle.

Keep writing, because you won't know who you really are until you see it staring back at you from the page.

Most people walk through life wearing masks. Writers don't. Writers tear those masks off with their books, to expose what's underneath.

I breathe books. I dream books. Books flow through my bloodstream.

Always believe in yourself. Don't let anyone drive you into the ground. Keep at it, and one day it will happen.

Every time I finish reading a great book, I wish I could stay in it forever.

I'm a phoenix. Burn me, I will keep rising.

Why writers stumble over words when talking? Because we have so much to say, our mouths can't keep up with our brains.

In your heart lives a gentle creature, your story. Let it spread its wings. Let it fly. WRITE.

Living life distracts from writing.
Writing distracts from living life.
Therein lies the conundrum.

Don't write to win, write to share.

Write when you're sad. Write when you're happy. Write when you're mad. Write when you feel crappy.

Bleed out your story. It's a painful process, but in the end you will feel lighter and we will feel enriched.

WRITE. And don't let the naysayers sway you.

Art is not about sweating over it in fear of it being stolen, it's about giving it away and collaborating with others to create more art.

In the sea of your thoughts lies treasure. Dive deep inside, discover it. WRITE.

Fear is the most debilitating
obstacle to creativity.

The longer you suppress it, the more it will eat at you from inside. Let your story out. WRITE.

No matter how strange your story seems, KEEP WRITING IT. We will all die out like mammoths if we stop sharing our stories.

Now that I'm an adult, I can finally be the kid I always wanted to be.

Art is everything.

Your dream won't happen if all you do is dream about it. Do it.

Stop trying to write a novel. Just tell a story, type it up, 1 hour every day, and by the end of the year, WOW! You'll have a novel written.

You know why I write? Because paper can't tell me to SHUT UP.

The more you write, the better you get. The better you get, the more you write.

Words have power. And in the hands of a skillful writer, words have power to change the world.

Don't just sulk. Sulk on paper.
You'll have a novel written before
you know it.

Write, write, write like mad.
Because you'll go mad, if you
don't do it.

I found the only way to get better at writing is to keep writing.

I'm fragile, you can break me with one word. I'm strong, I can break you with one word. I'm a writer.

Don't write for someone else, write for yourself, for your own enjoyment. That's when others will enjoy it too.

You think too much. Stop thinking.
Feel. Writing is about emotion.
Feel it, and it will flow.

Writers get paid for daydreaming,
so that others can daydream too.

Writing a book is like pulling strands out of your soul, one by one, until one day instead of a mess it finally looks like a story.

Your first words will be awkward, just like your first steps were awkward. But you can run now, right? So you'll be soaring in your writing.

Write. Write every day. Write utter shit. Write and make mistakes. But keep writing. It's the only way to get better.

Breathe. Believe. Write. Read. Repeat. Oh, and don't forget to dream. Dreams come true, you know.

Who says you're alone? There is the sky to hug you, the trees to whisper to you, the ground to hold you, the flowers to nod to you.

Don't let the world distract you. No matter what happens, keep working on your craft. Keep writing. Keep reading. Keep dreaming.

Write crazy stuff. Write incoherently. Write what to others reads weird, but to you makes sense. Above all, keep writing.

Reading makes me thirsty for writing. Writing makes me thirsty for reading. The cycle never ends.

If I listened to everyone who told me I can't write, I would've never even dared to start.

Write, and you might save someone's life. You never know.

Normal people go out on a Saturday night. I WRITE.

Who says writing is easy? Just try pulling your soul out word by word every day and not lose your sanity in the process.

If you have time to kill, don't. Read instead.

A writer is a genius not when critics say so, but when her or his book pierces your heart and rips off your blindness with its brilliance.

At any cost, finish writing your novel. You won't see how to make it better until you're fully done with it.

To write a good book, you must feel it. You can fake everything else, but not emotions.

If the writer's heart is not in the book, the reader's heart won't be in it either.

Read. Read everything and anything you can get your hands on. And then read some more.

I can't hide myself from you. My failures and my triumphs are out there for all to see. I'm a writer.

Don't listen to critics. Their job is to critique. You're a writer. Your job is to write.

Can't live without writing. Can't write without reading. Can't read without dreaming. Can't dream without living.

Write. Write even if you think it's shit. Write more shit. Write shit every day. Then one day you'll find yourself REALLY WRITING.

I want to bury my head in books like in pillows and breathe in stories like air.

Believe. No matter what anyone says, believe in your story. Write, and one day your story will help you believe in yourself.

Write. Write nonsense. Write the stupidest stuff you can come up with. Write about your socks, your cat, your aunt. JUST NEVER STOP WRITING!

No matter what anyone tells you, keep writing. Guess what, while they talk, you will crank out a whole novel.

The conundrum of writing is that you have to believe in yourself to write, but you have to write to believe in yourself.

Go crazy. Dig deep into your madness. Dance around like a lunatic. Grab handfuls of stars and eat them like candy. Live. Dream. WRITE.

Writing is not about stats, numbers, or selling. Writing is about touching that someone other with your words, to share your bliss.

Let's start a revolution, one word at a time. Let's write and not let anyone stop us.

WRITE. Because if you won't tell your story, who will?

If your heart is aching, it's because it wants to shed its pain. Let it. Write a story.

I don't know how to write, but I know how to feel, and that is what I write down.

They say your dialogue sucks? Keep writing. They say your plot sucks? Keep writing. They say your story sucks? KEEP WRITING NO MATTER WHAT!

Writers don't need food. Writers can survive on coffee, idea fumes, and trifles. Rich literary trifles.

There is a time machine. It's called, BOOKS.

Write. Not because they tell you, but because your stories will burst you apart if you don't.

Writing is like learning how to swim. The better you get, the less frantic you are, the more fluid and controlled are your movements.

I'm a writer. Ink is my blood. Universe is my brain. Fire is my heart. Paper is my realm. Books are my magic.

Be foolish. Be unpredictable. Forget about grammar and rules and every single writing advice you ever heard. Write from the heart.

WRITE. Because your heart alone can't hold your story.

WRITE. Write like mad. Write without looking back, before the doubt will set in and slow you down with its miserable whisperings.

Writers are immortal. They live on through their books.

Write your soul out. Your soul will thank you later.

Books are an enchanted interspace between reality and magic.

Don't worry about getting published. Write for therapy. Write for you.

To be able to write a novel you have to be willing to fall out of life for 1 year and not let anyone sway you.

Made in the USA
San Bernardino, CA
17 September 2016